"It is a blessing to have another collection of poems by Kilian McDonnell, his third in just a handful of years, and to find in it so many which speak with such clarity to anyone struggling to live an authentic spiritual life. Struggle and imaginative risk-taking are everywhere in these pages, both in the often gloriously subversive, scriptural understories characteristic of this poet, where we are taken inside the lives of anguished personae such as Hagar or Judas or Isaac—'And I must ask what kind / of deity is this who asks this horror, / whose will lies in the absurd / and in the abyss beyond?'—but also, and indelibly, in the vividly personal writing to be found in the third section of the book, 'At Dusk,' where poem after poem resonates with unprecedented depth of feeling and frankness of disclosure. With pieces such as 'Hiding,' 'The Wolf Will Wait,' 'Do You Love Me?' 'In Search of Trust,' 'Cosmic Lazarus,' 'Places I Have Rested,' and 'At Dusk,' to name a few, Kilian McDonnell, in laying bare his soul, has laid up some treasure for his readers, whose numbers will surely continue to grow on the appearance of this brave, revealing collection."

Michael Dennis Browne, Morse-Alumni Distinguished Teaching Professor of English University of Minnesota

"God's 'desperate love' strides through McDonnell's work; reading it becomes another reason to get up in the morning. McDonnell has heard the Scripture's female voice and, like a faithful scribe, responded 'Here am I' by writing down her intimacies. You'll love the sweet nectar in these poems, their earthy details, the humanness of the women and men who inhabit their rooms. You'll want to sit at Levi's table for his feast, and by the power in McDonnell's words and images, you can."

Sharon Chmielarz, author of The Other Mozart

"If what Simone Weil says is true, that 'unmixed attention is a form of prayer,' then *God Drops and Loses Things* constitutes a poet's breviary. Kilian McDonnell's pure attention to the astonishing events and telling details of familiar biblical stories enables him to re-imagine them in ways that surprise and delight the reader even as they instruct. In language that is both classic and colloquial, the voices of antiquity speak to us from these pages and include the likes of Adam and Abraham, Moses and Mary Magdelyn, Jezebel and Jesus, all of whom seem as near to us as the next room. Fr. Kilian, a lifelong Benedictine monk and a learned theologian, brings intellect and imagination to bear on this rich material and offers us glimpses of the wild wisdom of God's ways even as it eludes the speakers of his poems and the actors in the events of salvation history. The poems remind us that ours is a world in which 'splendor barges in' when we humans least expect it, in which 'God drops her hairbrush in the desert' on a regular basis and leaves it to the poet 'to hear it . . . and write it in a book.' In poems that are as brave as they are beautifully made, and as troubling as they are true, Fr. Kilian does just that, much to the reader's pleasure, over and over again."

Angela O'Donnell, Fordham University, poet and author of MINE

SAINT JOHN'S UNIVERSITY PRESS

COLLEGEVILLE, MINNESOTA

GOD DROPS
AND LOSES THINGS

Kilian McDonnell, OSB

Editor: Martha Meek

Cover layout by David Manahan, OSB.
Cover photograph by Simon-Hoa Phan, OSB.

Scripture texts in this work are taken from the *New Revised Standard Version Bible* © 1989, Division of Christian Education of the National Council of the Churches of Christ in the United States of America. Used by permission. All rights reserved.

Library of Congress Cataloging-in-Publication Data

McDonnell, Kilian.
    God drops and loses things / Kilian McDonnell.
      p. cm.
    Includes bibliographical references.
    ISBN 978-0-9740992-4-8 (pbk.)
    1. Bible—Criticism, interpretation, etc.—
Miscellanea. I. Title.
BS511.3.M335 2009
242—dc22   2008048233

For the Board of Directors
of the Collegeville Institute
for Ecumenical and Cultural Research,
present and past,

in gratitude for its unstinting stewardship
of the Institute's distinct ecumenical mission

CONTENTS

LET THERE BE LIGHT

ADAM'S VERSION

*So when the woman saw . . . that the tree was to be desired
to make one wise, she took of its fruit and ate; and she also
gave some to her husband . . . and he ate.* Genesis 3:6

I never win, before sin or after.
Body, soul, spirit she was in
and with my bone before I was Adam.

Male and female Yahweh created them.
God added nothing to that rib
except curves, sight around

corners, and nectar. When I see
Eve, I know I'm male. The first
miracle tells me who I am.

God saved perfection for the last,
afterwards was bushed, needed a Sabbath.
Perfection mastered me, not
by nectar, but by early lunch.

IN THE BEGINNING MERCY

I was a hidden treasure and desired to be known, so I created the world. From the Islamic tradition

The Lord God who created heaven and earth,
tamed mists and the disordered deep,
rummaged among astonishment and mirth
within the vaults to spill on voids and heap
vacancies with wonders. The Spirit/wind
wound through caverns of God's presence for hoard
to rain down in mercy before we sinned.
Let there be light, and rays of God's own self poured
downward. This, the Lord Yahweh said,
is good. I will do it again. For five days
the Lord emptied the chest as though to shed
in haste the gold saved from always.
    Whatever of mercy, whatever of worth must go.
    No glory is safe. All, all are cast below.

ON HEARING THINGS MALE

In the beginning when God created the heavens and the earth
. . . a wind from God swept over the face of the waters. . . .
Then God said, "Let there be light"; and there was light.
Genesis 1:1-3

Did the author of Genesis hear Yahweh's voice
like the rumble of thunder over Mount Zion?
And did the man say to himself, as though spitting
against the wind, this boom must be male?
Male ears hear things male. Even medieval giants
decreed, *Whatever is received, is received*
according to the mode of the receiver. And if
Yahweh drops her hairbrush in the desert,
who can hear it? And write it in the book?

FROM SARAH'S BOOK OF PROVERBS

I will incline my ear to a proverb. Psalm 49:4

If Abraham brags of my beauty to men, should I hear
only complaints of watery wine?
—If Lot says God made him to throw the spear in war,
did God create Milcah to wait for camels
carrying home the bodies of her sons?

If Leah has no part in the choice of her man, she can
drop goat dung in his wine.
—A man may read Akkadian and speak Attic Greek,
but can he bear the silence of Eve betrayed?

When Abraham obeyed God, I know there was horror
in his heart as he raised the knife to stab our Isaac.
—When Abraham shouts at me, it's because he's angry
at himself.

If your tent leaks, do not mend it in a storm.
—When Abraham and I quarrel, I cannot wait until
we smile and I breathe his breath.

If I have no sons and Abraham loves me, I weep
because it's not enough.
—When Abraham is sick, I berate Hagar.

If Aram grumbles of sour wine and burnt bread, let him
   sleep under a sheep skin too short to cover his feet.
—When Abraham is gone to war, I eat six times a day.

If an ant is lazy, the whole colony perishes.
—If Abraham neglects to say he loves me, let him
   consult the donkey.

If Peleg keeps dumb his wife Anna who milks the goat,
   he's a fool to think she knows only cheese.
—When Abraham is with me again, I grow taller.

If your dog wags its tail at everyone, do not set it to
   guard your gold.
—Men say wise women do not wear ankle bells.
   Why cannot we be wise and make music too?

If Abraham obeys God, what about God's command,
   Do whatever Sarah asks?
—When Abraham lies, God does nothing; when I lie,
   God reproaches me.

If Eve comes from the rib of Adam, every man
   afterwards passes through a woman's birth canal.
—When Abraham travels without me, wherever he goes
   is my home.

If God made Adam to plant the seed in the time it
    takes to saddle a camel, why did God make the seed
    grow nine months in Eve's good earth?
—If God tells Abraham to leave the graves of his
    ancestors, were the bones of my forebears buried
    too deep to mention?

If a man fells an oak, when its roots smell water it will
    sprout again.
—When he gave me to Pharaoh, Abraham got in
    return sheep, oxen, and slaves;
    God gave Pharaoh boils.

If Abraham is unjust to the shepherds, I will hate it,
    but woe to the wife who complains to me.
—When Abraham dies, I will die, and we'll be buried
    together so our bones touch.

FROM ABRAHAM'S BOOK OF PROVERBS

How long will scoffers delight in their scoffing and fools hate knowledge? Proverbs 1:22

If you spit at the sun, it does not get wet.
—If God says, *Go!* prepare to die in the desert.

If the rug merchant promises the red threads won't
    unravel, be ready to sleep on rocky ground.
—If you trust the Hittite on the age of that camel you
    bought, expect a viper to lick your fingers when you
    put them down its hole.

If you watch the maize seed sprout, remember it grows
    when you sleep.
—If God's promise is unfulfilled, it's still God's promise.

If you can build a bridge across a canyon, can you throw
    a rope to the moon?
—Perhaps you can endure a God who gives commands,
    but can you live with a God who says nothing?

If every falling rock is a threat to a handsome face, why
    pitch your tent near Yahweh's cliff?
—If my love for Sarah fails, so will the turpentine of the
    terebinth tree turn to honey.

If a fool shows you the way to the sea, you may never
    see water.
—If God leads you in darkness, will you ever see light?

If your camel walks fifteen days without water, do not
   beat the donkey because he needs an oasis twice
   a day.
—If pregnant Hagar reproaches barren Sarah, do not
   expect a quiet soup.

If the man alone decides to pass his son through fire,
   remember the same camel skin covers husband
   and wife in bed.
—If you climb God's mountain of glowing coals,
   expect the soles of your feet to burn.

If you believe there's good grazing on the far side of
   the country, do you want your sheep to die on
   the way?
—If you wrestle with Yahweh, beware of a knee in the
   groin.

If you have faith in God's promise of sons and lands,
   must you die this side of the mountain before you
   see either?
—If God makes a covenant in blood with you, why are
   you surprised to see your flesh upon the altar?

OWNERSHIP

Hagar

[Abram] went in to Hagar, and she conceived; and when she saw that she had conceived, she looked with contempt on her mistress. Genesis 16:4

My breasts do not sag like wet rags;
firm as unripe pomegranates
they will drip rich milk. Mistress,

you're nothing without a son.
Though rain falls in torrents,
you're sterile as the Dead Sea.

You think you're queen
and I should wait beside
your throne lest you forget

and drop a date pit. Things
are not the same, my dear.
I've tented where you tented;

he topped me. Now his great
son leaps in my belly
like a stag eager for wild places.

When I sweat upon the birth stool
I intend every tent in the desert
to hear my screams.

Sarah

*"I gave my slave-girl to your embrace, and when she saw
that she had conceived, she looked on me with contempt."*
Genesis 16:5

At first Hagar slept late like a Perizzite princess,
left the night crock full. Always hovering

over Abram: Master this and Master that.
Forgets I own her, and the baby's mine.

About to drop the kid, whines of aching
back, swollen legs, eats lemon cakes,

dates dipped in wine, and winks at passing camel
drivers. Pushes her spine forward to bulge her belly,

tacking right and left in front of me like an overloaded
pleasure boat in full sail on the Euphrates
thrusting ahead, zigzagging toward the rocks.

QUESTIONS FOR A BURNING BUSH

*Moses was keeping the flock of his father-in-law Jethro . . .
and came to Horeb, the mountain of God.* Exodus 3:1

No doubters live in arid sands
where demons dwell. I drive the flock
toward Mount Horeb in search

of pasture. No shepherd dares the dark
unknown gods of other nations who live
upon the peak. Why does Yahweh

lure me here? Why does any seeker's choice
condemn the chooser? Not to come
is mortal deficit; to come is mortal risk.

If Abraham should put no knife to Isaac's
throat on Mount Moriah, it's defiance.
To plunge the blade is murder. At Horeb's

base I'm drawn to see a burning bush
that does not turn to ash but speaks my name.
I'm repulsed by flames that invite me

to approach. Surely God cannot be like
the eucalyptus tree, with orange/red flowers
and leathery leaves of aromatic oil
whose decay poisons the ground beneath.

ISAAC AT THE ALTAR

"Take your son, your only son Isaac, whom you love, and go to the land of Moriah, and offer him there as a burnt offering on one of the mountains that I shall show you."
Genesis 22:2

God lies. I'm not my father's only
son. Why me? Ishmael's older,
his blood smells as sweet.

Men's lies bring us to a viper farm.
God's lies spring the cage door
open. Yahweh asks the God-mad

Abraham to knife his love, his hope,
sever the thread that binds logic
to life. And I must ask, what kind

of deity is this who asks this horror,
whose will lies in the absurd
and in the abyss beyond?

MIRIAM ON THOSE DAMN FOREIGN WOMEN

"I sent before you Moses, Aaron, and Miriam." Micah 6:4

Look, Moses, I was there, I didn't wander in
after the Exodus. When we sacked the gold of Egypt
I was bold as any; I grabbed pearls from the queen's
box, plundered silver plate from Pharaoh's pantry.
The pillar of fire went before the two of us. I strode
at your side through walls of waters Yahweh parted,
with you put my foot on Sinai sand. On the shore I sang,
horse and rider God has thrown into the sea. God
called me, sent me. When you bed an alien wife, I speak.
She flutters her eyes, you crumble. Are the daughters
of Sarah swamp toads that you must cuddle a woman
who never blooded door posts, never ate bitter herbs?
   Today you pillow a pushy Cushite.
   Tomorrow erect an altar to the lady's Baal?

THE IMITATION OF GOD?

When the LORD your God gives them [Hittites,
Girgashites, Amorites, Perizzites, Jebusites] over to you
and you defeat them, then you must utterly destroy
them. Make no covenant with them and show them
no mercy. Deuteronomy 7:2

Who parked Your well-greased
chariot of war in my oafish
genes? Made in Your *image*

and likeness, am I programmed
to maim all Hittites sauntering
through the maple grove to catch

the evening air? Am I
to imitate the God who killed
all firstborn in Egypt,

decreed: *Do not leave*
a breathing thing alive;
deposed disobedient Saul

who spared King Agag,
kept the best sheep and lambs
to sacrifice to You in Gilgal?

Yes, I own my shanty
by the sea, eat the bread
I bake, and an unsheathed dagger
slumbers in my bed.

DEATH OF A QUEEN

"The dogs shall eat Jezebel . . . and no one shall bury her."
2 Kings 9:10

Sweeping to meet her death, Jezebel
falls before the gods of sanctuary
psalms and orgies, alien queen

who did in Naboth for vines and lands,
killed prophets. From an upstairs window
she watches uncaged death charge

toward her as Jehu's dust whirls
across the desert. Slowly the Queen
turns to her toilette, bouffés

her hair to a tower crusted with rubies,
black eye-paint to cover collateral
damage, pearl choker filigreed

in gold. Lastly, the purple robe she brought
from Sidon, with cleavage like the gorge
down Mount Gilboa, monstrous sleeves

that billow then drag along the floor.
Yes, she whispers to the mirror.
The queen moves back, pauses as though

to greet a courtier kneeling in the mud
until she inclines her head, lifts
a forgiving finger. She strides to the balcony,

as Jehu drives into the court below,
the king's blood wet upon
his chariot wheels. *Scorn is authority,*

the queen murmurs to nobody. She calls
down, *Peace, is it peace you bring,*
you swamp of uric seepage? Jehu

shouts commands to her eunuchs who launch
her from the balcony, sleeves and skirts
swelling like sails in a northerly wind.

Chariot studs stamp until her blood
splatters the walls, puddles the ground.
The queen's poodles lap it up.

MYSTERIUM TREMENDUM ET FASCINOSUM

*I said: "Woe is me! I am lost, for I am a man of unclean lips . . .
yet my eyes have seen the King, the LORD of Hosts!" Isaiah 6:5*

Like Isaiah, I, too, have unclean lips, step back,
tremble before the Holy that draws me

close. What live coal must purify my mouth
when I answer to the Judge? Shall I

be judged by Law or by the Holy
which stands behind it? If I can choose

between edict and the bush that burns
unconsumed, I'll embrace the implacable Torah.

Any thug who stumbles
into court might escape between

see-through cracks in the 366 prohibitions
of the Law. If I have trouble living in history

with the Torah, where are the fissures in the Holy?
I do not speak of antiseptic rectitude,

but fire's absolute autonomy that scolds me
for putting dirty sandals on glowing cinders,
but invites me to approach barefoot.

PULLED FORWARD BY LIGHT

THE ROBBER ANGEL COMES

The angel Gabriel was sent by God to a town in Galilee called Nazareth. Luke 1:26

Thirteen, ignorant of angels, she stands
barefoot in the kitchen, garbage crock
overflowing. Splendor barges in, radiates

shadows. Mary draws back, raises her arms
to ward off attack; pulled forward by light,
she waits to be embraced, hears a voice

within the Splendor saying she's chosen to carry
an unwed mother's shame. The world waits
upon her nod. Mary takes in the light, scarcely

able to keep the glow in her belly. Splendor
vanishes. Years stolen, stooped as with hard
wood bundles on her back, alone in the dark.

JOHN IN PRISON

"I [Salome] want you to give me at once the head of
John the Baptist on a platter." Mark 6:25

In my cell I hear music.
The guard says Herod entertains;
Salome's doing her thing.

I'm cold. A prophet should see
the future, but I can't even see
tomorrow. I ranted my piece,

poured the water, wonder
now what it washed.
I pointed a finger at my cousin

and saw the Jordan roll off
his head. Whatever else
I doubt, him I do not.

God speaks to me
no more, so I watch the small
histories of other prisoners,

the green lizard and the fly.
A snap of the sticky tongue
and death by glue. I count

the cracks in the floor. All I hear
are camels grunting outside
my window and the music fading.

WIDOW RACHEL, MATCHMAKER

The Rabbis fixed the minimum age for marriage at twelve years for girls and thirteen for boys. Roland de Vaux, Ancient Israel, 29

I tell myself to leave that man alone. The time I've wasted on him I could have arranged fifty marriages to daughters of fifty fussy rabbis. When Joseph was alive I proposed the virgins of Rabbi Reuben, Rabbi Moshe, Rabbi Solomon—beauties too, slim of waist, strong of womb and limb and teeth. But Jesus Bar-Joseph would have none of them.

He's no recluse: decisive of movement as his large hand grasps an ebony mallet; assertive in selling his cypress benches—they're not cheap; barters hard at market for a chisel with acacia grip; with authority dominates the synagogue when reading the text of Torah, as though the words were his; inventive in scrounging fish and bread on travel to the temple; untiring at wedding dances as girls mourn.

When Joseph died I thought Jesus might change. Mary needs grandchildren. The man is thirty and still at home with mother, so, of course, the women whisper as they gather at the market stalls. A man without sons burns a page of the Torah.

I offer Naomi, daughter of Rabbi Levi, a girl a king would storm fortress walls to wed: long black hair caught at the neck in a silver net, skin the color of purest Sinai sand, deep set almond eyes full of promise, a smile that would crack the blackest volcanic rock. Sixteen, no jewelry needed, and she'd bring thirty goats. Jesus shakes his head, runs his hand along his cedar plank feeling its smooth grain.

BOTTOM FEEDERS

Levi gave a great banquet for him [Jesus] in his house;
and there was a large crowd of tax collectors and others
sitting at the table with them. Luke 5:29

Levi fluffs the tasseled
pillow behind the Master's
back, serves lamb, cooked figs

with almonds, quinces, camel
cheese, and Lebanon wine.
The first to recognize the prophet—

robbers, adulterers, tax
embezzlers—lift their wine
to toast the guest of honor.

Behind the Master, along
the wall, stand alley
stragglers who know no Torah,

come to see the prophet.
Peter and Andrew shift
on their goatskin couches,

though street talk does not fall
on unaccustomed ears. Men
fishing in the Sea of Galilee

are used to dubious catches,
coarse ambiguities. In dense
fog the hemp torch

on the prow sheds its light
as far as a man can throw
an anchor, the ship in danger

of falling off the ocean's edge,
and still they fish. From depth
beyond deep, the nets

dredge up bottom feeders,
fat on sea decay. But broiled
in garlic sauce, sour
wine, and honey, they're transformed.

MARY MAGDALENE, APOSTLE

*[Jesus] went on through cities and villages, proclaiming
and bringing the good news of the kingdom of God. The
twelve were with him, as well as some women who had
been cured of evil spirits and infirmities. Luke 8:1, 2*

I'm no slut. Never a come-on,
hand on hip, inviting
jacobs into bed. Out of our own

purses we women provided
the prophet's barley bread
and lentils. We strode beside

him, shook the same dust
from our sandals, spoke
kingdom to God's hungry.

My private household devils,
seven Beelzebubs to be exact,
rummaged in the noonday sun

among my modest ruins.
These he cast out with, *Go!*
On Easter he showed himself

first to me, spoke my name,
a sound my heart fed upon;
when I grasped his ankles,

I was afraid. Even love
could not hold him, flesh
standing in glory. Yet

he sent me, a woman, as apostle
to apostles with news
they would not believe.

GOD DROPS AND LOSES THINGS

*"What woman having ten silver coins, if she loses one . . .
does not . . . sweep the house, and search carefully until she
finds it?" Luke 15:8*

Like David belting to fight Goliath,
Miriam at market tightens her girdle
to haggle with the rabbi's wife,

who asks too much for her black beans.
She's so righteous—you'd think
she sleeps with Moses. At home

Miriam places ten Yehud drachmas
on the counter, each with Caesar's Roman
nose full in her Jewish face. All at once

only nine. Has she dropped one?
With her bramble broom she sweeps until
she finds it near the woodpile.

A lost silver coin's not nothing
in her house. To raise a cup for finding
what was lost, she calls across

the fence to the tanner's wife and the shepherd's
wife. They've shared her wine before.
Like the year her rebel daughter, Sarah,

ran away to a far country with a tavern
stud: chest of black hair, pimp roll,
and a camel driver's come-on smile.

Sarah's a fire-cat queen with claws,
no home girl. She likes clanging bracelets,
ankle bells, the danger of strangers.

The brave man gave her trinkets,
beat her black. Swollen jaw,
a cut above her puffy eye, she came

hacking back, a discarded consumptive
from his stable of harlots. Through the window
Miriam sees her three vineyards away.

She'd know that slouch anywhere, the way
Sarah shuffles. Out of the house Miriam
charges, runs down the road like a demented
lion to gather in her wounded cub.

PETER: CONFESSIONS OF AN ADOLESCENT

"And I [Jesus] tell you, you are Peter, and on this rock I will build my church." Matthew 16:18

I saw the prophet touch a leper, feed five thousand
with heels of bread and minnows, twelve baskets

left over, then come walking on the storm waves.
A green boy, I stood to walk upon raging waters,

high as cliffs at Herod's Masada. Four brave steps,
then a wave broke above, and doubt soaked me.

I sank like a rock, grasping for the hand that touched
the leper, gave bread and fish and life.

THE PRAYER OF THE IMPERTINENT

*"Even though he [the neighbor] will not get up and give him
anything because he is his friend, at least because of his
persistence he will get up and give him whatever he needs."*
Luke 11:8

A pounding on my door at midnight
    like kettle drums of coming wars.
        I'm in bed, children asleep,
            the latch is locked. This pest from down

the street keeps shouting to my upstairs window,
    Uncle Zachariah (rich Uncle Zachariah)
        has traveled at night to avoid the heat,
            arrives unannounced. I've no crust

for him to gnaw before he sleeps.
    I pull the patchwork blanket higher
        because he always has his hand out.
            This time I'll not be victimized.

Still the unforgiving thunder. (Is there no
    balm in Gilead?) I stumble arthritic
        arches downstairs to that bum at my door.
        Peace. A crust of bread for sleep.

At midnight who's got principles?

THE KING'S BANQUET

"The kingdom of heaven may be compared to a king who gave a wedding banquet for his son." Matthew 22:2

Bastards! With fat words
they accepted invitations to my son's
wedding banquet and now

that mutton's on the table, and expensive
wine from Cyprus this minute

poured, they send excuses. Ugly
Jacob, with seven ugly
bachelor sons, visits

disobliging parents of plain
girls left over from the marriage
market. Omer is off

to Arabia to buy prize
camels for stud . . .
Am I a Hittite hedge-king,

whose dominion extends for thirty
cubits from sty's edge
to Habab's scrawny bushes?

Quick boy, search the alleys,
scour back roads
for the breadless, limbless, eyeless.

Bring them to the banquet. If even then
some empty couches, run
to the thieves' dives, race

to the brothels and bring the jacobs,
madams and the wasted prostitutes. Compel
them to come in. I'm the king and when

I throw a banquet, I throw a banquet.

THE WOMAN WRESTLER WINS

[Jesus] said to her, "Let the children be fed first, for it is not
fair to take the children's food and throw it to the dogs."
Mark 7:27

Tired of bickering with scribes about clean/
unclean, he crosses the border
between Jewish lands and Gentile country
for the first time; only to call
a Greek woman *dog*,
you know the kind: little yapping
lap beasts with angry teeth.
She brushes off his words
as if swatting picnic flies.
And like a wrestler using her opponent's
weight against him, nails him
to the floor, instructs him
on the Kingdom of God: *This dog says,*
let the children be fed first,
but even dogs under
the table eat scraps
your children give them.
Like a woman erasing chalk
that marks the hem from upper skirt,
with her wet dishrag
she wipes away the line
dividing Jew from Greek.

AFTER SILENCE PANDEMONIUM

*Jesus entered the temple and drove out all who were selling
and buying.* Matthew 21:12

Caiaphas said: *What prophet climbs
the temple stairs, waits a moment*

*mute at the gate like a king surveying
his estate? As if the jaws of hell had opened*

he shouts Desecrators! *at hawkers, lashes
with a whip, scatters bleating sheep*

*among the godly, upturns the shekel tables
sending Passover pious on their hands*

*and knees. He breaks open cages
of squawking birds, doves fly free*

*dropping silvery globs, a sacrificial bull
lunges, women scream, children wail,*

*priests swear obscenities. He himself
desecrates the temple.*

THE LEAP OF FAITH

Jesus on the night when he was betrayed took a loaf of bread. 1 Corinthians 11:23

After bitter herbs, I place
upon the table my strange bread
and wine, a really hard

saying. Wise men are wary
of this leap over a fisherman's
tally of the catch, a tax

collector's pinch of each
extracted coin. The apostles are
accustomed to the logic of ripping

sails and strong boxes
for Caesar's drachmas, but I lure them
into *Because I say it.*

When they look down,
no solid ground beneath them,
except my hand upon the table.

JUDAS RECEIVES THE BODY OF CHRIST

So when he had dipped the piece of bread, he gave it to Judas son of Simon Iscariot. After he received the piece of bread, Satan entered into him. John 13:26, 27

Judas takes the bread I dip
into the wine, extend across

the table. He knows I know,
but won't betray him. A twisted

heart, no doubt wanting
a different kingdom. When he eats

my body, a dark presence
enters him and I must let

my Judas go. I urge
my friend to act quickly.

Before we say the last prayer,
sip the last cup of wine

he slips into the black night
and scuttles toward the temple.

He once loved me, loves
me now. I grieve for the companion

who stood beside me when Lazarus
stumbled from the tomb.

SUDDENLY THEY VANISH

Then all the disciples deserted him and fled.
Matthew 26:56

My chosen suddenly gone
—spring rain turned brackish
in the race through the wadi—
unstrung boys I'd foolishly
asked to keep the northern

hordes at bay. Not an untaught
choir, as though I gave them
angular, metallic music
to sing sight unseen,
to fall apart like tone-deaf

strays. Have I botched it?
They lost not the apocalyptic
battle on the mountain against
dark principalities and powers,
but the first skirmish on level

ground facing temple guards.
I bring this sour wine to you,
Father, see you swirl it
in the chalice, lift it to discerning
lips, drink with infinite desire.

FOOL'S WISDOM

For Jews demand signs and Greeks desire wisdom, but we
[Christians] proclaim Christ crucified . . . the wisdom of God.
1 Corinthians 1:22-23, 24

We soldiers seize him in Gethsemane,
nail him to a tree. And when we raise
him to his throne, we think of Maccabean

warriors and deaths of little consequence,
like slitting throats of geese. A Greek king,
wanting to uncircumcise the Jews, ordered

they forget Torah and temple as though discarding
worn-out shoes, decreed they eat Greek
meat and, failing to convince a Maccabean

mother and her seven sons to feast
on piglets, tore out their tongues, their scalps,
cut off their feet. Finding Jewish faith

still not collapsible, he fried them in a pan
like quail. His soldiers called the Maccabeans
dumb to die because of pork chops,

as we say of the king we whip, strip,
nail, stab, genitals exposed
—a meat-ax debasement befitting a dirty Jew.

CRIMINAL BLOOD

[When the soldiers] came to Jesus and saw that he was already dead, they did not break his legs. Instead, one of the soldiers pierced his side with a spear. John 19:33-34

I raise my spear to pierce the heart
of the Jewish fraud and hear low

moans of women watching at a distance.
Blood spurts upon my hands and breastplate,

like the burst of wine when the spigot's
ripped from the barrel. Scum die

each day, red runlets pollute the gullies
and no one comments except to curse

the swarms of flies. Like table wine,
blood is cheap. Stray dogs

lick the base until the dripping stops.

THE PALIMPSEST ON CALVARY

There were also women looking on from a distance. Mark 15:40

Then all the disciples deserted him and fled. Matthew 26:56

But all his acquaintances, including the women, . . . stood at a distance, watching. Luke 23:49

I read histories to find that truth's
a palimpsest; holding it to the light
one sees erasures, words rubbed out
beneath the text. On Calvary Mark

could find no apostle, who'd sworn the night
before to die with Him, only women
who'd made no vows. Matthew knew
the apostles ran down the mount

with a sack full of reasons. Later Luke
erases the indictment, scrapes away
the scandal, overwrites the history too harsh
to hear; *acquaintances and women stood*

at a distance. The bloody truth: men
gave him up to bloody death, were nowhere
near the hill, while women, embracing
one another, stood fast and wept.

CUR DEUS HOMO?

"One man [must] die for the people." John 11:50

Never one to leave a mystery
at peace, unfingered,
I bounce the unknown against

the unknowable and get only
the notes of my footnote game.
What dark necessity, I ask,

decreed that he must stretch
his arms, Romans pound the nails?
A medieval monk in Gaul

—looking up from his Aristotle—
said because some ass stole
a bag of wormy pears,

some king at evening soup
knifed an unsuspecting potentate
who turned his head to check out

the queen, and God, foreseeing
all from all eternity, deflected
righteous wrath upon the Son

and he must die.
Actually, I know much less
and Anselm's syllogisms cannot gain

a purchase on the why of God
—a barbed-wire silence.
Could it be that Jesus

didn't know why?
So I and other reprobates
could go to God, he bent his knee

to the Father's dread, unfathomable decree
written with a switchblade
dipped in blood and desperate love.

THE BEGGAR COMES AT MEALTIMES

*Later he appeared to the eleven themselves as they were
sitting at the table. Mark 16:14*

The door locked, we're mouthing Passover
lamb scraps. James raises a cup
of therapeutic wine. Before we drink,
a light so intense we gasp, like stepping
off a cliff, or the rush of mad love.
The master we saw die naked
two days ago, now beside the bread
crusts and dirty dishes, presto,
garbed in white brighter than the sun, hands
outstretched for bread crumbs like a beggar.

He always comes when meat and Esau's
mess of pottage are on the table,
as though banqueting in paradise
on manna the archangels baked
is too gauzy, table talk too expurgated.
Up there no biblical bickering,
no one filches drachmas from the purse.
No one in the boat doubts when waters rage
or asks for resurrections from the dead.

Above, no brassy sons bring pushy
mothers to grab the thrones beside the king.
The cock need not crow.

Why then does he come?
Mercy hungers for our treacheries.

THE TOP OF THE TABLE

*"No eye has seen, nor ear heard, nor the human heart
conceived, what God has prepared for those who love
him." 1 Corinthians 2:9*

Father Dennis, a hundred and one,
stops shouting for the night
nurse, gasps, and dies,
going to the untouchable, unknowable

God forever. Here
I'm not in danger of my certainties,
but Boethius is probably right:
eternity's the full possession

of life always present
in totality. But that's as untouchable
as God. In the banquet hall
we cannot taste the spread

upon the high table: silver
candelabra, Beluga caviar,
fennel bulbs, Drunken
Goat Cheese, truffles

found where lightning strikes,
Barolo Mascarello wine
from Piedmont ($195.30),
and the pantry's not empty.

QUESTIONS OF THE DYING

"Listen! I [Christ] am standing at the door, knocking; if you hear my voice and open the door, I will come in to you and eat with you, and you with me." Revelation 3:20

Am I, poor fool, one of those
who think the time in the *corrida*
has come when gates open

and a great black beast turns
to face me, and I have no sword,
no *muleta* to deceive the brute,

although God shouts *Olé*? If a speck
of polonium is enough to kill in a London
café, what was in that cup of water

the nurse just gave me? Are my stones
bruised and hammered enough
to build the New Jerusalem with its streets

of gold, transparent as glass?
Am I Odysseus's dog, who alone
can recognize his master in disguise

when he returns to Ithaca after twenty years?
The mutt, too weak to raise his head,
too old to wag his tail, dies of joy.

AT DUSK

FATHER'S FEDORA

In family photos always the old fedora,
small red feather in the sweat-stained band,
at every gathering of the clan. He never

groused about being dead. Problem was
hospital gowns, bedpan fuss, catheters,
oxygen tubes. Death will erase

memories of broken bats, bases
loaded, wet towels. Why not
locker room champagne forever?

The going should be quick, clean.
Not the mess of stepping into fresh
cow pies with out-of-date white shoes

in Velva's Wild Wood Park,
where red oaks hold crisp
wrinkled leaves through Dakota winters,

to drop in April. No one sees
them fall. No one rakes them
for burning. Suddenly they're gone.

But it was nothing so clean as the April
day the feather in father's fedora fell
and Dad stooped down and never rose.

I VISIT THE BONE HOUSE

"There is no one who has left house or brothers or sisters or mother or father or children or fields, for my sake and for the sake of the good news, who will not receive a hundredfold now in this age . . . and in the age to come eternal life." Mark 10:29-30

I come from Jerusalem to the monastery Justinian built in the mists of Sinai's Jebel Musa, where Yahweh spoke Torah to Moses. Monks still sing loud praise when everyone's asleep, plant vines for wine, sow barley, bury their dead.

They enshroud the dead—still warm—in regulation grey, the blanket off his bed. It takes time in the earth for the last fat worm to lick clean the leg's *quadriceps femoris*, eat all the marrow, collapse on the sternum, die full of days. After the bones spend ten years in the dirt Abbot Moses orders Brother Sabas to dig them up, place them in the charnel shack standing outside the cloister, convenient as an outhouse.

He takes me to the shack, opens the pitted door, unpainted since Justinian. Neat piles of brown craniums, tibias, femurs, vertebrae and stray black teeth. No flesh, no stink. But a tangy sweet bouquet like honeyed balsamic vinegar.

We monks visit the shack to be reminded of the decay and splendor racing toward us; you visitors, formaldehyde and glory.

Some monks believe if we search, we find and touch God's face—on the farther side of faith. Love's the thing. Others say fear's essential to climb God's mountain.

In that heap of dry death lies Abbot Arsenius—died a thousand years ago. He mopped latrines, let no monk doubt God's wrath. Abbot Paphnutius—went to school with Clovis—taught much is uncertain, much we do not know, except God's in the mercy business. Brother Isaac, the Syrian—flourished as Mohammad turned toward Mecca—believed holiness's something God does, fasted to the bone, died ferret-faced and laughing, took only half a blanket to lower him below.

Brother Sabas locks the door, but death is not bolted.

THE CATHOLIC THING

The carnality of the [Catholic] Church really drew me.
Mary Karr

Catholicism isn't for lotus eaters:
we put a body on the cross.
Like all dysfunctional families
We tear flesh, spill blood
                              before we eat.

To celebrate the naked Christ between
the thieves: jeweled crosses, purple
cassocks, lace cuffs, ermine capes.
Popes and bishops draw the line
                              at rouge.

We're big on things we can touch:
wine, bread, oil, votive candles,
and, sometimes, the palpable
body of man. The Word made flesh
                              weeps.

MACULAR DEGENERATION

Some rusty pipe inside
bursts, spilling spent blood

upon the macula,
blots out the light.

Neither time, nor space,
nor mass, said Einstein,

are true constants;
only light.

Why then this black
hole? Sure,

God, like yeast,
transforms by corruption.

Yesterday I was indestructible
eighteen, the sea

was deep; today
decaying in the shallows.

HIDING

How long, O Lord? Will you hide yourself for ever?
Psalm 89:46

Had I looked in the exhausted
church, a blind groper
clicking the floor with a cane?

You were not in the candle
or in incense clouds. Nor
in the black book of psalms.

Though you promised, you
promised, not in the taste
of thin bread—it was not

sweet on the tongue or sweet
in the heart—Not in the taste
of the cup I breathed upon.

Empty silence in corridors
and cell. So I sit beneath
the maple with a blister on its trunk,

branches broken by a storm.
Someday I'll be found.

THE WOLF WILL WAIT

Unless a grain of wheat falls into the earth and dies, it remains just a single grain. John 12:24

By some animal within-ness,
forest-bred, uninstructed,
I sense a presence following me.

Has Yahweh stepped upon a twig,
like a careless wolf, startling
deer, losing supper?

I turn to see. Nothing.
I know Yahweh's back there,
scent and traces

on the forest floor, a broken
cedar branch, a crushed
leaf. I can know

a little—but not enough.
Stalking me the great
wolf waits until I'm weak.
Where death, there God.

DO YOU LOVE ME?

"My God, my God, why have you forsaken me?"
Mark 15:34

Some stupid pistol picked off
the street lights on rattlesnake

alley as I stumble over shards,
walking to Your palace. Nothing's

the same. When I come to Your well,
my thirst is gone. The edge

of Your word no longer cuts,
the altar bread like cardboard.

Bone-cold, needing more love
than I deserve, I seek Your fire.

You share your hearth with stragglers,
lost children, lost sheep. You send out

charred goat from a failed sacrifice,
while I wait outside Your gate.

IN SEARCH OF TRUST

I know the one in whom I have put my trust.
2 Timothy 1:12

Up the street of dying
ash I mount the cemetery
hill to face Kacmarcik's
looming cross.

Last winter I fell
three times on glassy ice
(nearly broke my hip)
placing scraps of marinated

beef beneath the oak
to tide my fox through freezes
of Minnesota winter.
(After a year I found

I was feeding crows.
This monk draws the line
at crows.) At eighty-seven
I guard my *ralentando*

days, but they go. Did I
misplace them, like my
yellow pills? Or did some crows
snatch the marinated days

from beneath my acorn-less oak?
Anyway, they're gone.
Soon, soon, I mumble
at Aelred's new mound.

Yesterday I was twenty-one.
As I pass Godfrey's grave
I wonder what straw he grasped,

where he put his trust.
Where mine?

COSMIC LAZARUS

We know that the whole creation has been groaning in labour
pains until now. Romans 8:22

We tread on dirty snow up the path
beside the dirty frozen lake
—acid soot from chimneys—
to piles of sod and pebbles we'll throw

upon the coffin. Each time
we walk the cemetery tarmac,
I ask the dead *Is this it?*
Always the pastor answers *No,*

with that maddening collared certitude he gets
from talking long to God. *There's*
more. Creation screams in labor
and the Spirit brings forth one

undivided splendor in the risen Lord,
in risen us, and in the risen universe,
chains forged before God invented
time or made the water wet.

The damaged Savior pours his treasures
as though some deranged god has
blown up the dike, loosed ungovernable
seas. Our preposterous God with a preposterous

love will not take us unless nebulae,
whales, Mount Hood, the four
rivers of paradise and the Mississippi
come along. I smell hope

as a farmer in spring sniffs new
rain before it falls on parched
fields of winter wheat and barley.

VIOLIN AND PILLOW

Arnold Dittberner, OSB, 1907–1999

Three times he breaks his hip,
three times refuses to die.
Who says life is tenuous?

No marrow in the brittle bone,
wheezing from a tubercular lung,
he breathes on. A twig of a man,

with an appetite to founder
a stallion, on his back
praying an oversized rosary.

Never a well day,
beloved by pharmacies.
Suddenly he dies beside

the violin he scratched for joy
(threatening a concert), next to
the round black pillow,

hole in the middle,
he carried to monastic meals
and psalms for southern pain.

AUSTRALIA

Angelo Zankl, OSB, 1901–2007

He slouches over his desk
(bottle opener, dice, rosary)
reaming out four pipes,
soot on the floor,
tamping down tobacco from his twelve cans.
At 103 should not smoke;
I've buried all the brilliant doctors.

Talks to nurse Teresa about the joys of heaven:
If you want a T-bone steak and you're in Australia,
                              you'll get it.

Enthusiastic about parties,
chess less so, since Nancy beat him.
I can't believe I lost to that woman.

Birthday April 19, 2003.
God forgot me. But that's okay.

Scratches in his journal.
November 10, 2004:
Cyril visited me 10:30 a.m. Nice monk.
Anne (she's so sweet) brought me un-sugared orange
                              juice 10:46 a.m.

Read torn National Geographic *about anacondas in*
                              the Amazon 11:03 a.m.
Abbot John stopped in. Looked tired. Nice abbot.
                                              2:45 p.m.
Lights out 9:30 p.m.

Nice day.
No sleeping pills for Angelo.
A can of Killian's Irish Red 9:30 p.m., 12:30 a.m.,
                                              4:00 a.m.
At 10:30 p.m., 1:30 a.m., and 5:00 a.m.:
Help! Help! I've got to pee.
O thank you, dear.

July 12, 2007, 4:31 p.m., Angelo, 106, departs for
                      Australia to eat his T-bone steak.

PLACES I HAVE RESTED

God saw everything that he had made, and indeed, it was
very good . . . and he rested on the seventh day.
Genesis 1:31; 2:2

I can rest any place, dear friend,
although I have my preferences, lairs

much visited. I rest in Seamus Heaney,
bog-lover, prodigal who remembers home,

chaste as the pope in a pub, language
lush crowned king. In that miser

Emily Dickinson, who counts the night's
small coins to see no word is overspent,

each berry pinched until it bleeds.
In Robert Hass soliloquizing on

swans, cats and blackberries,
caressing vowels for the long embrace.

In *Die Meistersinger*—six hours
of Germanic glory—a lot of culture

in sausage, beer, boney knees,
lederhosen and busty maids.

In Joe Turner, who invented light,
splashed it across the channel ships

—I never knew the sun could breathe.
But I rest best in wild canaries

outside my monastery window, tiny
fallen suns, frantic out of orbit, flashing

a wilder yellow in search of their gods.

AT DUSK

Up the hill
between lake and window

come fawn and doe.
They see me, but stand

beneath the dead
oak unafraid.

Does the wild know
something the old monk

forgets? I move
and they are gone.

NOTES ON THE POEMS

Page 18. "*Mysterium tremendum et fascinosum*" is based on the book *The Holy* (1917) by Rudolf Otto. The full German title is *The Holy: On the Irrational in the Idea of the Divine and its Relation to the Rational.* Central to Otto's idea of the holy is the numinous, that is, mystery, which elicits from the beholder terror (*tremendum*) and fascination (*fascinans*). The numinous both repulses and attracts. For Otto, the numinous was a nonreducible original category.

Page 30. "Peter: Confessions of an Adolescent" was written at a reunion of the McDonnell family at Tamarack Lodge in Seeley Lake, Montana, August 4, 2005.

Page 39. "Fool's Wisdom." The artistic tradition has depicted Jesus on the cross with a loincloth. Jesus may have been crucified covered, though the ordinary way the Romans executed criminals was to nail them naked. However, Pontius Pilate, in deference to the sensibilities of the Jews, may have ordered a loincloth. This seems unlikely in view of past rulers trying to break down Jewish culture and identity (1 Maccabees 1:41-61), such as introducing Greek gymnasia in which athletes compete naked (1:14), an affront to the Jews. Pilate's rule as prefect of Judea was generally calm. On the other hand, he and Rome had little regard for Jewish feelings, saving public order. No other prefect had dared to place the sacrificial symbols of pagan cult (diviner's rod and libation vessel) on the coins of Judea, a considerable offense to Jews who had to use them. It is unlikely, then, that he would depart from Roman practice of crucifying criminals naked out of consideration for Jews. Further, the intent of the Romans was not only to kill but to shame and degrade. For Cicero crucifixion is "that most cruel and disgusting penalty."

From the biblical text itself one cannot determine between nudity and loincloth. But Melito of Sardis (died about 190 CE), one of the great theologians of Asia, visited Jerusalem about 160, approximately 130 years after the death of Jesus. Possibly from what he learned of the Jerusalem tradition he was able to write in a homily (*On the Passion*, 97): "The Master has been treated in a disgraceful fashion, his naked body not even deemed worthy of a covering that[his nakedness] might not be seen."

Page 42. "*Cur deus homo?*" This Latin phrase is the title of a book written by Anselm of Canterbury (1033–1109). Literally it means "Why did God become Man?" But as used in Anselm's book it has a wider meaning, namely, why did God become man and fall under the necessity of dying on the cross? In the earlier centuries some thought that Jesus had to die in order to pay ransom to Satan, who had acquired some rights over humanity by reason of the fall of Adam and Eve. Anselm rejected this view and proposed to replace it with the idea of satisfaction. Sin, being an infinite offense against God, required an infinite being to bring satisfaction equally infinite. It was necessary for God to take the place of man and make complete satisfaction to divine justice. Many theologians no longer accept Anselm's theory. "*Cur deus homo?*"presents a different view.

Page 51. "I Visit the Bone House." The recollections of my visit to St. Catherine's Monastery in the Sinai desert thirty-four years ago may not correspond to the physical facts. The monastery was constructed by Emperor Justinian about 550 CE and is the oldest active monastery in the world preserved almost completely in its original state. Justinian had it built around what was thought to be Moses' Burning Bush. Tradition has it that the mountain towering over it is the place where Moses received the Torah. One of the major texts of the Bible, Codex Sinaiticus, was discovered in the monastery in 1850. Also, it houses the second largest collection of illuminated manuscripts (the Vatican has the largest). Because it contains a Mosque within its walls it was not plundered by Moslem invaders, and therefore it is the depository of priceless art of an antiquity not found elsewhere. Today most of the monks are Greek.

Page 54. "Macular Degeneration" was written at a reunion of the McDonnell family at Tamarack Lodge in Seeley Lake, Montana, August 12, 2006.